Becoming
a Victory Girl
Staking Your Claim in the Kingdom

Amy Elaine Martinez

amy
elaine

DEDICATION & ACKNOWLEDGEMENTS

This book is dedicated to all the *Victory Girls* who are braving the battlefield of Life to defend their territories and stake their claim in the Kingdom of God.

Thank you to my sweet husband, David, for championing my dreams and waiting on me to grow up into a *Victory Girl* who could love you the way Christ intended. You taught me about lasting love before you even knew the Lord. Since you've met Him, it's been amazing to watch you grow, trusting the Lord in all things. I love you. Thank you for being patient…always.

I want to thank my boys, Sidney and Gabriel, for bringing me to my knees in prayer over so many things. You make me trust the Lord *a lot*. I love being your mom and I'm so proud of both of you. You make me laugh more than you make me cry…that's good right? The two of you are the reason I wanted to become a *Victory Girl* and a *Victory Mama*! One day, I hope to be helping y'all raise up some *Victory Grand-Girls*!

A special thanks to my parents, Gaile & Carlton Ward. Mom, you're the reason I'm so in love with the Word. You showed me how to be a *Victory Girl* before I knew it was possible. I've watched you pour over the Scriptures my whole life. Thank you for your steadfast prayers that saw me through my *crazy*. Daddy, you are an incredible example of the Father-heart of God. You are the most generous man I know.

A huge thanks to my sister, Molly Gaile Jenkins. Molly, I'm so glad you're alive! You're the ultimate *Victory Girl;* you cheated death! I love you for so many reasons. You've encouraged me every step of the way in my writing journey. You continually inspire me to live each day to the fullest.

To my daughter-in-love, Riley, you're the reason I began writing books and walking in my calling. I wrote my first book for you when you were just a Bride-to-Be. You've blessed me in so many ways. I finally got my girl and you're definitely a *Victory Girl*! I love how you love Jesus and my first-born!

Thanks to my core group of friends, *The Girls*, who carried my dreams when I couldn't or wouldn't believe in myself. Y'all made me brave enough and courageous enough to try new things. Because of you, I began to walk fully in my God-given destiny. Specifically, I want to thank Betsy, Karla, and Paula because you've been telling me for years I should be doing this *writing thing*. I'm so glad I finally listened and took that first step into the unknown two years ago. Thank you for your mentoring, support, and love. Y'all are absolutely *Victory Girls* and I love doing life and ministry with you!

I also dedicate this book, in loving memory, to my brother, John Carlton Ward, you left us much too soon. Losing you brought me closer to God through my *further still* moments. My faith was fortified as I walked through the grieving process. It was a very long year where I learned to trust the Lord *even if* I didn't understand.

All of you are the reason I continue to write. Without family, friends, and my faith, I'd have nothing to write about. Thank you for inspiring me in your own unique ways. I love you all.

Finally, my deepest thanks goes to the One who made me a *Victory Girl* by dying on the Cross in my place. Jesus, because You rose from the dead, I'm free. You made me brave enough to fight my biggest battle, the one that rescued me from my own selfish heart. I'd be nothing without Your love. Thank you, Holy Spirit, for Your transforming power that made this broken girl whole again. Abba Father, You're such an amazing Papa. Thanks for letting me sit at Your feet, cry my eyes out, ask the hard questions, and find the courage to keep pressing in for more of You and less of me. You are the reason I am a *Victory Girl*!

CONTENTS

INTRODUCTION

Becoming a Victory Girl: Staking Your Claim in The Kingdom will help you fully walk out your destiny in the Kingdom of God.

By waging war and training for triumph you'll discover how to:

- Suit up for battle, get your brave on, and walk in confidence as *Warriors of Victory*

- Pray with power, authority, and accuracy, hitting the mark every time by mastering *The Art of the Aim*

- Stake, claim, and keep the territory you've conquered while *Staking Your Claim in The Kingdom*

- Bask in *The Bounty of the Battle* as you take back what the enemy's stolen

By the time you finish this book, you'll be more confident about:
- Your Spiritual Inheritance
- Your Spiritual Identity
- Who's really fighting your battles

Most importantly, you'll know how to become the girl you were always meant to be, a *Victory Girl*.

At the end of every chapter, you'll find some *basic training* designed to help you as you train for triumph. Waging war against the enemy isn't an easy task. Becoming a *Victory Girl* isn't for the faint of heart, it takes lots of dedication to BATTLE, BECOME, and BELIEVE! These sections will help you believe God and become a *Victory Girl*. As you battle it out, become who He's made you to be, and believe God's Word, you will begin to see yourself as a *Victory Girl*.

WARRIORS OF VICTORY

God, your God, is right there with you, fighting with you against your enemies, fighting to win. Deuteronomy 20:4 The Message

Becoming a *Warrior of Victory* through Christ is possible. You can do this! *Becoming a Victory Girl* will help you live out a victorious life! My hope is you'll walk away feeling victorious, refreshed, passionate, and poised in the pursuit of your enemies. Perhaps, you'll even feel a little invincible, knowing God, who is called Faithful and True, really is Who He says He is!

Outnumbered and out-armed. Surrounded by fear and shouts to "Surrender!" Waging war on every front. This is the sacred battleground of Life. Sounds like a movie scene, huh? But, no, this is just another day where chaos threatens and trials are thrown like grenades barely missing us. We stare wide-eyed as the battle rages on.

Lately, I've been feeling a little worn out from the endless battles I'm fighting. How about you? Are you feeling outnumbered? Feeling like you can't get ahead in the fight of your life? Left feeling battle-bruised, desperately defeated, and weary from waging war? Perhaps you're feeling deserted, helpless, hopeless, and forgotten by the One who claims to be Faithful and True...the One who said He'd never leave you nor forsake you?

Although we may *feel* all of those things, we can't rely on our feelings alone. We must learn to set aside our feelings and cling to our faith. When tempted by emotions and feelings, the truth of God's Word must be the plumb line on which we stand. Making rash, hasty decisions shows we are not trusting Him completely. Yet, when we utterly rely on God, our chaotic choices change to carefully thought out acts of obedience. This is where we begin to live in victory!

Self-confident know-it-alls will prove to be fools. But when you lean on the wisdom from above, you will have a way to escape the troubles of your own making. Proverbs 28:25-26 (TPT)

He who trusts in his own heart is a fool, but whoever walks wisely will be delivered. Proverbs 28:26 (MEV)

Aren't we all looking to be delivered from these "light and momentary troubles" that are supposedly producing glory within. We want out; it's human nature! And, if we can't be delivered, can't we at least be made strong for the battle?

Yes, we can.

Wisdom can make anyone into a mighty warrior, and revelation-knowledge increases strength. Wise strategy is necessary to wage war, and with many astute advisers you'll see the path to victory more clearly. Proverbs 24:5-6 (TPT)

Moses was both a hard-headed and deeply emotional guy. Yet, God taught him how to successfully wage war using faith to trump his emotions and ultimately experience victory. He can teach us too! Using God's Word as the standard for our faith, leads us to victory.

With God on our side, we can face our battles standing on flourishing faith not our floundering feelings.

In Deuteronomy 20, God helps Moses set up the *Rules of Warfare*. He says when you go to war and you feel outnumbered, don't be afraid; remember Who is fighting on your behalf.

"When you go out to battle against your enemies, and see...a people that outnumber you, do not be afraid of them, for the Lord your God is with you..." Deuteronomy 20:1 (MEV)

When we're feeling outnumbered, we must stand on the truth and remember what Hebrews 13:8 tells us, "God is the same yesterday, today and tomorrow." Remembering the goodness of God and His faithfulness helps to keep our eyes fixed on the *God of Angel Armies*. Recounting the times God's shown up for us in the past strengthens us for the battles ahead.

In Deuteronomy 20 and Ephesians 6, the Bible gives us some excellent advice on how to go about the business of waging war against the enemy of our soul. If we can keep these things in mind, we'll win one of the biggest battles we'll ever face, the battle with ourselves. You know, the one that ravages our mind. We're often our own worst enemy. And, who needs another enemy? I sure don't.

WISDOM
can make
anyone a
MIGHTY
WARRIOR.

Proverbs 24:5 (TPT)

The Bible teaches us some wise strategies and helpful truths for engaging in victorious warfare in Deuteronomy 20. Some of the most helpful are: Unfinished business leaves you distracted. Before going into battle, make sure you've finished what you've started; the battle before you needs your full attention. Unresolved fear and feelings of intimidation are both easily seen by the enemy and also highly contagious to those around you. Before the battle, put on the full armor of God, suit up, and encourage yourself in the Lord.

Don't waver in resolve. Don't fear. Don't hesitate. Don't panic.
God, your God, is right there with you, fighting with you against your enemies, fighting to win. Deuteronomy 20:1-4 (MSG)

Let "Peace!" be your first battle cry. If possible, avoid the fight. If an attack ensues, sweep the land of all that is unholy and take the spoils, the plunder. In the spiritual realm, this means gather up all the blessings of the battle: the confidence, the victory, the deliverance, *and* the territory. Take ownership and be sure to carry them with you into the next fight.

In a long battle, cut down the obstacles in your way and use them against the enemy. But, if those obstacles can produce fruit (love, joy, peace, patience, kindness, goodness, faithfulness, gentleness, and self-control) in you, don't cut them down, fight your way around them. They will provide life-sustaining food for your soul and your future.

This is just the beginning of learning how to fight and win!

WARRIOR WORDS: A Warrior of Victory knows when she needs to send out for reinforcements. We aren't meant to fight our battles alone. Knowing when to call a friend or come running back in retreat are vital lessons to be learned. However, when we find ourselves feeling all alone on the battlefield, we can cry out to Jesus with the *Victory Girl's Battle Cry*!

THE VICTORY GIRL'S
BATTLE CRY

I never fight alone.
God fights for me.
He goes before me and behind me;
He never leaves my side.
God has made me strong for battle.
I have everything I need
to fight and win.
I am a Victory Girl!
I am victorious
in Christ!

God is strong, and He wants you strong. So, take everything the Master has set out for you, well-made weapons of the best materials. And put them to use so you will be able to stand up to everything the Devil throws your way. This is no afternoon athletic contest that we'll walk away from and forget about in a couple of hours. This is for keeps, a life-or-death fight to the finish against the Devil and all his angels. Be prepared.
You're up against far more than you can handle on your own.
Take all the help you can get, every weapon God has issued,
so that when it's all over but the shouting you'll still be on your feet. Truth, righteousness, peace, faith, and salvation are more than words. Learn how to apply them. You'll need them throughout your life. God's Word is an indispensable weapon. In the same way, prayer is essential in this ongoing warfare.
Pray hard and long. Ephesians 6:10-18 (MSG)

If God is on our side, then tell me: whom should we fear?...But no matter what comes, we will always taste victory through Him who loved us. For I have every confidence that nothing—not death, life, heavenly messengers, dark spirits, the present, the future, spiritual powers, height, depth, nor any created thing—can come between us and the love of God revealed in the Anointed, Jesus our Lord.
Romans 8:31, 37-39 (VOICE)

There is only one strong, safe, and secure place for me; it's in God alone and I love him! He's the One who gives me strength and skill for the battle. He's my Shelter of love and my Fortress of faith, who wraps himself around me as a secure shield. I hide myself in this One who subdues enemies before me!
Psalm 144: 1-2 (TPT)

PRAYER:
Father God, teach me how to fight my battles with bravery and confidence. Make me a *Warrior of Victory.* Give me strength for each new day. And, when I'm weary from the battle, let me find my rest in You, Jesus. You are my Shelter of love and Fortress of faith. Thank You for surrounding me with Your favor like a shield.

BATTLING IT OUT

What's your current motivation for reading this book and why do you want to pursue becoming a *Victory Girl*?

Think about your biggest battle; what strategies and truths from this chapter can you apply to help you be victorious?

How would being a Warrior of Victory make you more successful in the battles you're facing today?

Choose 3 ways you are going to battle it out to become a *Victory Girl*.

Write out *The Victory Girl's Battle Cry* on a notecard, put it somewhere you can see it, say it out loud, rewrite it in your journal, and try to memorize it. Speaking out the truth is one our most reliable weapons against the enemy. Try this battle cry next time you're under attack.

BECOMING STATEMENTS

With God on my side, I can face my battles standing on flourishing faith not my floundering feelings.

Recounting the times God's shown up for me in the past strengthens me for the battles ahead.

BELIEVING THE BIBLE

Don't waver in resolve. Don't fear. Don't hesitate. Don't panic.
God, your God, is right there with you, fighting with you against your enemies,
fighting to win. Deuteronomy 20:1-4 (MSG)

With God
on our side,
we can face
our battles
standing on
flourishing faith
not our
floundering
feelings

Thanks be to God!
He gives us
the victory through
our Lord Jesus
Christ.

1 Corinthians 15:57 (NIV)

THE ART OF THE AIM

Prayer is essential in this ongoing warfare. Pray hard and long.
Ephesians 6:17-18 The Message

What do chicken nuggets and princesses have to do with powerful prayer? I was about to get schooled. After a long week with my husband out of town, I spent a Friday night hanging out with my then, eighteen year old son, Gabriel. We ate chicken nuggets and watched an animated movie featuring a very brave princess. I had forgotten how much I loved this movie. Confession: Being the mom of two boys, I'm secretly hoping I'll have a few grand baby girls. And, since I have a redhead, it's possible one might look like the feisty princess in this movie. I also secretly hope both my kids have a spunky, confident girl-child as payback for when they were strong-willed, rambunctious little tykes. What I thought was just another entertaining evening to distract me from a difficult week, turned out to be a revelation of spiritual truth all dressed up as a princess.

The princess in this movie is a quick-witted, willful, redheaded beauty! Her name is Merida, which means, "one who has achieved a high place of honor." I truly believe there's a Merida in each of us!

We can be brave because we've been given everything we need to face our battles and be victorious. Let me say that another way.

You've been given everything you need to be a *Victory Girl*!

Every spiritual blessing in the heavenly realms has already been lavished upon us as a love gift from our wonderful heavenly Father… Ephesian 1:3 (TPT)

The weapons we use in our fight are not made by humans. Rather, they are powerful weapons from God. 2 Corinthians 10:4 (GW)

Girls, we have supernatural weapons; they're hand-made by God, ready for use, and at our disposal. We must learn how to wield them with supernatural strength. Each one of us has been given the arrows needed to shoot down our enemy. If we will employ three wartime strategies, we'll hit our mark each and every time. Victory starts by learning *The Art of the Aim*.

We begin by mastering these three *Victory Girl Skills*:

1. AIMING with the ACCURACY of the Word of God
2. STANDING in full AUTHORITY as daughters of the King
3. RELYING on the Holy Spirit for our ACUMEN

Acumen? What in the world does that mean? Acumen is the ability to make good judgments and quick decisions, typically in a particular domain or place. What a perfect description of what we call in the spiritual realm, *discernment*. Acumen is discernment. Because we have the Holy Spirit living inside of us, we have the ability to discern things in our God-given domain. We have the spiritual eyes to see the schemes of the enemy and pray against them.

Prayer should be our weapon of choice.

Now, in the natural, I've never shot an arrow in my life. But, in the spiritual realm, I've become an experienced archer. I've learned to draw back my bow and shoot my arrows right into the enemy's camp.

Our sweet princess has too! She faces an age-old dilemma of her day; she's about to be betrothed. The first-born sons of the neighboring clans have been summonsed to a competition of skill and strength. While they may not win her heart, one *will* earn her hand in marriage. However, this princess is not one to play by the rules. She's a free-spirited and rather athletic girl who decides she'll compete in this contest and conquer them all. She's fearless and determined. And, of course, she chooses archery as the winning game for her hand. She says something like, "I'll be shooting for my own hand today!"

She's practiced all her life to become an expert in archery. While her mom says a princess really shouldn't have weapons, her dad feels differently. Her father, the king, says, "Princess or not...Learning to fight is essential!" The princess had learned to defend herself. She knows she's skilled. She's mastered the *Art of the Aim*. But most of all, when the enemy comes after her, she knows, without a doubt, she's got the king watching her back.

Like our princess, we've achieved high places of honor through Jesus Christ. We are daughters of the King and He's got our back.

Our part is to learn to send out our arrows with precision in powerful, purposeful, and productive prayers. Learning to pray prayers that will produce the result and outcome we desire takes practice and perseverance. We can't be faint of heart if we want to become a *Victory Girl!* Our strategy? *The Art of the Aim.* We've been given a quiver full of arrows to defend ourselves against the enemy. Practice builds the strength needed and develops the accuracy required. Practice. Practice. Practice.

My question: What are God-worshipers like? Your answer: Arrows aimed at God's bull's-eye. Psalm 25:12 (MSG)

We must think like a warrior to become a *Victory Girl.* With love and truth wrapped around our weapon, we can take our aim. It may, however, take a paradigm shift in our mind to assume the right position. If we want to see God work in our lives, we must be still.

Surrender your anxiety! Be silent and stop your striving and you will see that I am God. Psalm 46:10 (TPT)

Our position in the battle is with the Lord before us as our shield, beside as our strength, and behind us as our rearguard.

Finally, receive your power from the Lord and from his mighty strength. Put on all the armor that God supplies… take a stand against the devil's strategies. Ephesians 6:10-11 (GW)

While we must learn to take a stand, our battles are best fought on our knees. There's a very real war going on in the spiritual realm. Our most powerful weapon is praying God's Word. How do we wield this weapon at the enemy? We must practice our aim to develop accuracy and precision in our skill. Before we know it, we'll be hitting the mark every time and bellowing out our victorious battle cry, "Bullseye!"

Our prayers are like arrows bringing heaven down to earth. When our will aligns with His, God hears our prayers and acts on them bringing breakthrough in our circumstances. Jesus taught the disciples to pray in this way, "on earth as it is in heaven." That's the kind of prayer the enemy does not want us praying. Fortunately, we can come boldly before the throne asking God to move heaven and earth on our behalf.

The *Victory Girl* is brave and prays big prayers!

ARROWS FOR YOUR QUIVER: Discernment develops your acumen. Spirit-filled prayers are powerful. Knowing your identity ignites your authority. Never forget, you are a daughter of the King. Scripture assures accuracy because God's Word shoots as straight as an arrow.

Shoot your fiery arrows and rout out the enemy!
Psalm 144:6 (VOICE)

Here He stands! The Commander!
The Mighty Lord of Angel-Armies is on our side!
Psalm 46:11 (MSG)

You, O Eternal, are the One who lays all good things in the laps of the right-hearted. Your blessings surround them like a shield.
Psalm 5:12 (VOICE)

The heartfelt and persistent prayer of a righteous man (believer) can accomplish much [when put into action and made effective by God—it is dynamic and can have tremendous power].
James 5:16 (AMP)

PRAYER:
King Jesus, I want to be your *Victory Girl*!
Teach me to fight the good fight and prepare my hands for the battle before me. May my arrows shoot straight, striking the enemy right in the heart. Thank you for going before me and behind me in every one of my battles. May your truth be my guide and your favor surround me as a shield.

BATTLING IT OUT

"You've been given everything you need to be a *Victory Girl*." Do you really believe that statement? Is there something you *think* you are lacking in your fight against the enemy? Stop right now and ask God to help you believe He's given you everything you need. Ask Him to stir up the gift of faith in you right now. Ask Him to make you brave.

How did the image of prayer being like an arrow bringing heaven down to earth make you feel? Spirit-filled prayers are powerful. Pray Psalm 51 today. Ask God to create a clean heart in you; ask Him to align you heart with His. Spend some time praying about the battles you are facing.

How would mastering *The Art of the Aim* make you more successful in the battles you're facing today?

Choose 3 ways you're going to *practice your aim* to help you become a *Victory Girl*.

Write out one Bible verse from this chapter on a notecard, put it somewhere you can see it, say it out loud, rewrite it in your journal, and try to memorize it. Using God's Word as an arrow helps you aim directly into the enemy's camp. Repeat this verse out loud the next time you're feeling under attack.

BECOMING STATEMENTS

Prayer should be our weapon of choice.

I'm a daughter of the King and He's got my back!

Our position in the battle is with the Lord before us as our shield, beside as our strength, and behind us as our rearguard.

BELIEVING THE BIBLE

Every spiritual blessing in the heavenly realms has already been lavished upon us as a love gift from our wonderful heavenly Father… Ephesian 1:3 (TPT)

"You must not only
AIM RIGHT,
but draw the bow
with all your
MIGHT."

Henry David Thoreau

"Faith is to prayer
what the feather is
to the arrow."

Thomas Watson

STAKING YOUR CLAIM IN THE KINGDOM

All the ground that you march over will be yours. Your territory will extend from...the south to...the north, and...in the east to...the west.
Deuteronomy 11:24 (GNT)

Sometimes God allows us to see things in the natural before He reveals the deeper spiritual revelation in the supernatural. On a recent flight, just before landing, I glanced out the window and snapped a picture. For some reason, the land intrigued me. The territorial lines were clearly marked and the individual parcels of land caught my eye.

After touching down, I headed home from the front-lines of my most recent battle. A few weeks later, I began to more completely understand my intrigue and fascination with the land. As God opened my eyes to get a glimpse of the way He see things, an expectation and anticipation grew deep within.

Still nursing my battle wounds, I spent time with the Lord trying to figure out what was going on in my life. What was this stirring inside of me? It was then, He opened my ears to hear the first rumblings of that still, small voice in my soul. As, I began to listen more intently...I began to hear the Lord saying, "Take the Land."

Somewhat confused, my response, my prayer, was something like this..."Take the land? What does that mean, Lord? I feel like I've been in a all-out war; I don't even know why there's a battle. What am I fighting for, what's at stake? Help me understand; show me what You want to me to learn...please, give me a strategic battle plan."

Power and might are in Thy hand so that no one can stand against Thee.
2 Chronicles 20:6 (NASB)

My destiny, my inheritance, my land were all at stake! I needed a plan! I needed it fast! So many questions; where to find the answers? A *Victory Girl* knows where to go to find the answers.

The best and most strategic planning for our spiritual battles can only be found in God's Word.

27

I began to ask questions like, "Who had victory in the Bible?" "Who took their land and kept it?" I needed to know. A *Victory Girl* asks the hard questions and listens when He speaks.

I found myself in 2 Chronicles in the Old Testament. In the Bible, the chronicles or annals of the kings include the historical accounts of the sometimes gory battles fought over territories and lands in ancient times. I found kings on the front-lines of the battlefield vying for their land. These kings were contending, fighting, struggling, *and* victorious. How did they do it? What was their strategy? How did they reign victoriously over their God-given lands? And, most importantly, how did they *keep* the land they fought so hard to take back from the enemy?

After hearing the news that a great multitude was coming against him, Jehoshaphat's first response was this:

Shaken, Jehoshaphat prayed. He went to God for help...
2 Chronicles 20:3(MSG)

Jehoshaphat's first-line of defense was to go to God and ask for help. That's exactly where we should head when we're facing battles in unknown territory. We'll find our way, when we get on our knees. His prayer is beautiful; he was crying out to God to make a way.

"When the worst happens—whether war or flood or disease or famine—
and we take our place before this Temple (we know You are personally present
in this place) and pray out our pain and trouble, we know that You will listen
and give victory."
2 Chronicles 20:9 (MSG)

I love how this version reads, *pray out our pain and trouble*. We can confidently go before the Lord and *pray it out*. He hears and He answers. We know every battle is the Lord's; and as New Testament believers, our victory has been assured through the work of Jesus Christ on the cross. He makes us ready for the fight when the enemy threatens to take over our land and ravage our territory.

Suddenly, I saw it! A strategic battle plan began emerging right out of the pages of my favorite book, the Bible. I knew I would find it there, and I'm so glad I knew where to look. God's promises always prove true. And, not only does He give us guidance, He strengthens us for battle too.

For You clothed me with strength for the battle. Psalm 18:39 (MEV)

Being a boy-mom and having home schooled my youngest, I love a good book. The Old Testament is filled with adventure and suspense. It gives us inspiration for the everyday battles we face in our lives. If you read the whole story of Jehoshaphat's victory over his enemies in 2 Chronicles 20, you'll see what I mean. It's exhilarating to see how God showed up for His people. And because He never changes, we know He'll show up for us too.

Victory Girls fundamentally believe in victory!

We have to believe in victory, if we want to remain hopeful and be strong enough to stake our claim in the Kingdom.

It's inevitable. There will be a battle(s) in this life. We will find ourselves on the front-lines of the battlefield in our quest to defend our territory and take our land. We all have a spiritual territory that's assigned to us. It's our God-given parcel of land that He staked out for us before the foundation of the world. The themes of inheritance and provision are strewn all through the Bible from Genesis to Revelation.

This land is rightfully ours, but we must be proactive and claim it as our own. We must stake our claim in the Kingdom. This is where the conflict begins, where the battle-lines are drawn, and where we must step out onto the front-lines. It's our inheritance. If we want all that the Lord has for us, we will have to fight the enemy to possess our land *and* inhabit it; not just visit like it's a vacation time-share, but *live* in our promised land.

The warfare surrounding our quest reveals that it is *indeed* part of our inheritance. The enemy doesn't want us to have all that Christ died to give us. Every time we go to battle, new territory is opened up to us. For every inch, there's a battle raging. We are sure to endure some pain and walk away with a scar or two. However, it is our responsibility to take our land and learn how to keep it.

THE VICTORY GIRL'S BATTLE PLAN
FIRST-RESPONSE, TURN TO GOD
BE HUMBLE
WORSHIP
GATHER YOUR TRIBE AROUND FOR SUPPORT
TRUST GOD FOR THE VICTORY
GIVE THANKS
REST/STAND

I can hear you now…"What? Rest? That's *not* a battle plan! Did I miss something?" Nope, you didn't, that's the way God works. His ways are different than our own. His battle plan is strategic and it looks nothing like the enemy's. If we'll surrender our way to the Lord's, there is joy, reward, victory, and peace to be had. Let's look at how Jehoshaphat's battle turns out and learn a little bit more about *The Victory Girl's Battle Plan.*

Even today, God gives specific words of instruction to us. When Jehoshaphat and his people called upon His name, the Spirit of the Lord showed up in the form of a *prophetic word,* saying,

"Do not fear or be dismayed…for the battle is not yours, but God's…You need not fight in this battle, stand and see the salvation of the Lord on your behalf…for the Lord is with you."
2 Chronicles 20:14-17 (NASB paraphrased)

After humbling himself before the Lord in worship, the king and the people stood up to praise God in a loud voice. They gave thanks to the Lord for His lovingkindness. As soon as they began singing and praising, the Lord took action to ensure their victory.

At the very moment they began to sing and give praise, the Lord caused the (enemy's) armies…to start fighting among themselves.
*2 Chronicles 20:20 (NLT) *parenthesis mine*

Can't you just hear them shouting, with fists pumping in the air, "Victory!" Their enemy had been utterly defeated. God had shown up just as He promised He would. He always does. You can count on His faithfulness. He never leaves us alone; He's a promise-keeper.

In the aftermath of the battle, we see Jehoshaphat and his people working tirelessly for three long days gathering their spoil. This is an important piece of the battle plan. We have to put in some elbow grease to get all the reward. There was an abundance, more than they could even carry; yet, this work was an act of worship. It was the Lord's provision for their days ahead. *This* job, *this* task, was from the Lord. It required their immediate attention to make sure nothing was wasted. This insightful nugget is so telling of God's heart for us… their work was completely acceptable to the Lord. Finishing this task before *formally* giving Him thanks was absolute obedience.

Sometimes we have to do the hard work immediately after a battle, but God sees it as worship. You can bet they praised Him while they worked, and we can too. On the fourth day, they named the valley where the battle had taken place, the Valley of Beracah, meaning *blessing.*

With God on our side, our battlefields become our valleys of blessing.

In the end, they all returned from battle with great joy, for the Lord had made them to rejoice over their enemies. They gathered at the Lord's house and corporately worshiped Him with thanksgiving and praise. This spoke volumes in the heavenlies. Our praise is loud in the spiritual realm and our worship is deafening to the enemy. Their surrounding enemies were filled with dread for they knew that the Lord had fought for His people. Rest and peace were established.

So the kingdom of Jehoshaphat was at peace, for his God gave him rest on all sides. 2 Chronicles 20:30 (NLT)

God wants us to "Take the Land." It's ours; we have a right to it. It's our responsibility to walk out each step of our territory, claim it as our own, rout out the enemy, and establish our residence there. Often, this will require a new level of confidence, awareness of our authority, and a strategic battle plan to keep the enemy out for good.

Taking the land requires answering two important questions:

1. How will I defend my territory?
2. His plan or mine?

Victory Girl, put your marching boots on and let's head out for a new frontier. Our land is ready and waiting for us to come and stake our claim in the Kingdom. The first step is the hardest, but you can know God's right there beside you. Remember, we were never meant to fight alone; gather your tribe, and get your brave on!

Wherever you set foot, that land will be yours. Your frontiers will stretch from the wilderness in the south...in the north, and from the east to...the west.
Deuteronomy 11:24 (NLT)

But thanks be to God who gives us the victory through our Lord Jesus Christ!
1 Corinthians 15:57 (GNT)

Jehoshaphat addressed his people with these words:

"People...Put your trust in the Lord your God, and you will stand your ground. Believe what His prophets tell you, and you will succeed."
2 Chronicles 2:20 (GNT)

The *front-line* is military terminology for the position(s) closest to the area of conflict formed by the most advanced tactical combat units; or the most advanced or visible position in a field or activity. This, sweet girl, is where the action happens!

For the Lord your God is bringing you into a Good Land...where you will lack nothing...there you will eat and be satisfied and bless the Lord your God for the Good Land He has given you. Make sure to love the Lord your God, walk in all His ways, and remain faithful to Him.
Deuteronomy 8:6-10 (NIV, paraphrased)

What's the key to keeping your land? Obedience, faithfulness, and a devoted heart after God.

Unfortunately, if you finish reading, you'll find idolatry crept back into the land. We must be aware of any "high places" set up in our lives and tear them down immediately, lest we fall prey to the enemy. It's a continual process. No one wants to go back onto the battlefield to regain the hard-fought territory they're occupying. Staking our claim and keeping our territory are daily battles, but we can keep the enemy at bay. Some days, we won't even notice him; other days, it'll be an all-out fight to keep him off our land and out of our territory.

CLAIM STAKERS: Put your foot down. Be a Claim Staker and kick the enemy off your turf. Be vigilant. Make no mistake, he's messing with a daughter of the King and the King's got your back! Let the enemy know *you know* exactly who you are in Christ. Use *The Victory Girl's Battle Plan* and watch your enemies scatter!

The LORD will grant that the enemies who rise up against you will be defeated before you. They will come at you from one direction but flee from you in seven. Deuteronomy 28:7 (NIV)

PRAYER:
Thank you, Lord, for my Good Land!
Help me to walk out every bit of territory You've set aside for me.
Make me ready to stake my claim in The Kingdom.
I want every bit of my inheritance.
I want to walk in my full destiny in You.
Teach me how to not only *take the land*, but to *keep* it!
May I keep praising You every step of the way.
Make me brave, Lord.
Make me Your *Victory Girl!*

BATTLING IT OUT

Think about this part of *Staking Your Claim in The Kingdom* and ask yourself these hard questions...

Taking the land requires answering two important questions:

1. How will I defend my territory?
2. His plan or mine?

How do you feel about being on the front lines of your battle?

How can *Staking Your Claim in The Kingdom* help you start walking in your full destiny today?

How will you keep the Good Land He's given to you? Take some time and come up with a battle plan of your own. Then, take the first strategic step in staking your claim. Tell someone about taking your first step; it will help you keep your brave on when the battle gets tough. Accountability always helps us win our battles because we're often tempted to give up. A good friend will keep telling you, "It's gonna be worth it all." They'll also help you continue fighting for your dreams and your territory. Make sure you have some good, Godly girlfriends to do life with and wise, Godly counsel around you.

Choose 3 ways you can stake your claim and become a *Victory Girl.*

Write out *The Victory Girl's Battle Plan,* keep it somewhere you can see it, say it out loud, use it in your Bible journaling, and try memorizing it. Using God's method for waging war against our enemy helps us remember Who's fighting on our behalf. Practice using this battle plan the next time you're feeling under attack.

BECOMING STATEMENTS

With God on my side, my battlefields become valleys of blessing.

BELIEVING THE BIBLE

For You clothed me with strength for the battle. Psalm 18:39 (MEV)

The Lord is my chosen
portion and my cup;
You hold my lot.
The lines have fallen
for me in pleasant
places; indeed, I have a
beautiful inheritance.

Psalm 16:5-6

The Victory Girl's Battle Plan

- first-response, turn to God
- be humble
- worship
- gather your tribe around for support
- trust God for the victory
- give thanks
- rest/stand

BATTLING FOR THE BOUNTY

Then I'll punish their slave masters; your offspring will march out of
there loaded with plunder. Genesis 15:14 The Message

You may be wondering what's the point of all this warfare. You
might be asking yourself the same questions I found myself asking in
the process of becoming a *Victory Girl*. Questions like: What's the
take-away? When we walk victoriously out of battle, what have we
actually gained? Is it just another W in a lifetime of battles we face or
is there something more? What about battling for the booty, the
bounty, the spoils, the plunder? The answer: Yes, there is more.

There's bounty in every battle.

God's Word confirms that when we engage the enemy, we won't
walk away empty-handed. There is much more than a Victory to be
had; there's an abundance of blessing. We were made for more. More
than occupying our territory and routing out the enemy, we were
made to take back what's been stolen from us. And as a bonus, we get
to gather up the bounty left on the battlefield as provision for our
next assignment.

Our covenant relationship with God ensures we are not only His
children, but we are co-heirs with a mighty big inheritance too.
Covenant, in the Bible, is a really big deal. God takes it very seriously.
The Lord's covenant with Abram is one of the first times we see the
concept of inheritance attached to our faith.

And Abram believed the Lord,
and the Lord counted him as righteous because of his faith.
Then the Lord told him, "I am the Lord who brought you out of Ur of the
Chaldeans to give you this land as your possession."
Genesis 15:6-7 (NLT)

Within God's plan, there is this idea of being *brought out* from one
place in order to be *brought in* to the place God has set aside for us.
God continues in this text by telling Abram that while His people *will*
face slavery and bondage, they won't walk away empty-handed.

I love that so much! We never walk away empty-handed from our battles! There is always something to glean and a blessing with our name on it. It's always worth our while because God never wastes a thing. He takes our ugliest battles and makes something beautiful; He calls it a *blessing*.

But, I will punish the nation that enslaves them, and in the end they will come away with great wealth....So the Lord made a covenant with Abram that day and said, "I have given this land to your descendants." Genesis 15:14, 18 (NLT)

Other translations use words such as plunder, many possessions, or many riches. The idea is that the enemy incurs a payback for all our years of enslavement. There's retribution for the harm done. The ideas of inheritance and the bounty of battle are seen from Genesis to Revelation. Many times, in the Old Testament, we see God's people gathering the bounty and spoils after a hard-fought battle. And, in the New Testament, we're encouraged; though we will have troubles in this world, there's a reward and victory attached to every battle fought. We will face suffering, but God tells us to be brave.

There's more to come: We continue to shout our praise even when we're hemmed in with troubles, because we know how troubles
can develop passionate patience in us, and how that patience
in turn forges the tempered steel of virtue, keeping us alert for whatever God will do next. In alert expectancy such as this,
we're never left feeling shortchanged. Quite the contrary—
we can't round up enough containers to hold everything
God generously pours into our lives through the Holy Spirit!
Romans 5:3-5 (MSG)

And what's more...

Jesus said, "The world will make you suffer. But be brave! I have defeated the world!" John 16:33 (GNT)

There won't enough backpacks to haul out the abundant blessings from our battles. If we scour the land we've just conquered, we'll find more than just a victory. We will find blessing, reward, favor, and inheritance. There's provision in the battle; it sustains us going forward. The things once used against us will now be for our benefit.

The best discovery I made while studying to write this book is this: God doesn't waste a thing. He uses every weapon used against us to build strength, stamina, and confidence deep within our souls. And in the process, He ignites a passion in us for more of Him. We begin to see that the battles are worth the bounty we carry off the battlefield.

God is well-known in the land… He is famous… making His home… living here on Mount Zion. That's where He smashes every weapon of war that comes against Him. That's where He uses the broken arrows as kindling for His mighty bonfire.
Psalm 76:1-3 (TPT)

Jesus said, "And how I long for every heart to be already ablaze with this fiery passion for God!" Luke 12:49 (TPT)

The weapons that once wounded become the kindling that sets our heart ablaze.

Our wounds are healed through the transforming power of the Holy Spirit, resulting in a passionate love and devotion to our Lord, Jesus Christ. For every hurt, every scar, every battle wound, He uses the purifying power of the Holy Spirit's fire to set a bonfire in our hearts, burning up what is not from Him and igniting a flame that burns for all to see. He's so good. He takes the very things used to harm us and works them out to demonstrate His glory in us that others might see and know He is God. It's all for His glory, to make Him famous. What seems so overwhelming now will one day be forgotten.

The little troubles we suffer now for a short time are making us ready for the great things God is going to give us forever.
2 Corinthians 4:17 (NLV)

When we're fighting for our inheritance and our territory, the condition of our heart matters to the Lord. It's often in and through the battles that He does a mighty work in our hearts. We've seen His mighty hand at work in our lives and it stirs up a new passion in our hearts for Him. The very things the enemy hurled at us are burnt like an offering of sacrifice and praise. We come away with a little ash on our faces, but oh so beautiful for the work He's done in our hearts.

God has sent me to give them a beautiful crown in exchange for ashes, to anoint them with gladness instead of sorrow, to wrap them in victory, joy, and praise instead of depression and sadness.
Isaiah 61:3 (VOICE)

Two things happen when we finally emerge out of a fierce battle:

1. The Lord uses the weapons that once wounded us as a kindling for the fire He ignites in our souls.

2. Others may or may not be able to see the changes in our hearts right away, but the Lord sees!

And He will say of us, "That one, she has a different spirit in her. She passionately followed Me into the fiercest of battles. She's my *Victory Girl*." Eventually, as He declares this over our lives, others will begin to notice what the Lord has done in us. When they ask about how we made it through, we can say, "Passion led me here!"

Look at what He said of Caleb's heart when he was about to step into his Promised Land. But my servant Caleb—this is a different story. He has a different spirit; he follows me passionately. I'll bring him into the land that he scouted and his children will inherit it. Numbers 14:24 (MSG)

Like Caleb, we have a different spirit. In the New Covenant, we've been given the Holy Spirit. He is living *inside* of us. The Spirit is like a fire burning within to keep us fighting the good fight. When the world asks us how we press on through our battles, we can wholeheartedly say, "It was passion that led me here."

What once made us insecure will now be the source of our security. What once sapped us of our strength becomes the very thing that stirs us up and brings us joy. What ate our lunch, now feeds our soul. What once caused fear brings about an unshakable confidence.

How does this happen?

"Not by might nor by power, but by my Spirit," says the Lord Almighty.
Zechariah 4:6 (NIV)

What's our bounty in the battle? Confidence, joy, passion, and victory. We walk away with imperishable things, refined by the fiery trials we endure. See, while we may feel stripped bare when we walk off the battlefield, we never walk away empty-handed.

We know this because of the covenant God made with Moses. God used Moses to lead the Israelites out of their slavery and into their promised land. He brought them out to bring them in. For years they were held captive in the enemy's land, but God heard their cries of distress. He knew of their suffering and sent someone to rescue them. God sees our suffering too. He sent Jesus to set us free from the things that enslave us. While addiction and oppression may have once held us captive, it is for freedom that we've been set free.

Christ has freed us so that we may enjoy the benefits of freedom. Therefore, be firm [in this freedom], and don't become slaves again.
Galatians 5:1 (GWT)

We don't have to live that way. We have every weapon needed to fight even our fiercest battles. After gathering the bounty off the battlefield, we begin to realize we have so much more than just natural resources. In Him, we have supernatural weapons; weapons forged by the very hand of God. The enemy's weapons have been rendered useless against us and we have victory through our faith in Jesus Christ. It's part of our inheritance for we are children of God and co-heirs with Jesus Christ. All that is His is now ours. Because our victory comes from God, we can confidently follow after Him.

When we passionately follow Christ onto the battlefield, we become a *Victory Girl*.

No weapon that has been made to be used against you will succeed. You will have an answer for anyone who accuses you. This is the inheritance of the Lord's servants. "Their victory comes from Me," declares the Lord.
Isaiah 54:17 (GWT)

Because of this inheritance, we can praise Him even in the midst of our battles. We can trust that with God at our side, our battlefields will become our valleys of blessing. We can look ahead with confidence. We can celebrate even when we think we can't stand the heat of the battle one more second. Because of God, we don't quit.

Our inheritance is incorruptible; it can't be taken from us. New life. New territory. Battle bounty. Victory. It's all ours for the taking. We've fought hard for it and it belongs to us. You might just say we get to have our cake and eat it too! And, that's a sweet reward!

So we're not giving up. How could we! Even though on the outside it often looks like things are falling apart on us, on the inside, where God is making new life, not a day goes by without his unfolding grace. These hard times are small potatoes compared to the coming good times, the lavish celebration prepared for us. There's far more here than meets the eye. The things we see now are here today, gone tomorrow. But the things we can't see now will last forever.
2 Corinthians 4:17-18 (MSG)

BOUNTY BUILDERS: Weapons that once wounded become the kindling that sets our heart ablaze. Bounty abounds on the battlefield. Troubles today are territories of triumph tomorrow.

O taste and see that the LORD is good: blessed is the man that trusteth in Him.
Psalm 34:8 (KJV)

Lord, I'm bursting with joy over what you've done for me! My lips are full of perpetual praise. I'm boasting of you and all your works, so let all who are discouraged take heart. Join me everyone! Let's praise the Lord together. Let's make him famous! Let's make his name glorious to all. So listen to my testimony: I cried out to God in all my distress and he answered me! He freed me from all my fears! Psalm 34:1-4 (TPT)

Those who passionately pursue the Lord will never lack any good thing.
Psalm 34:10b (TPT)

For every child of God defeats this evil world, and we achieve this victory through our faith. 1 John 5:4 (NLT)

PRAYER:

Lord, You are so good to me, transforming the weapons used against me into a fire burning within. May I passionately follow You wherever You lead…even into the fiery trials and the ongoing battlefields of life. Set my heart ablaze and teach me to take every bit of bounty from my battles. Thank You for being my portion and reward. I remain confident that I will see Your goodness here in the land of the living. I will stand on my promised land with hands held high in praise because I am Your *Victory Girl*!

BATTLING IT OUT

Think about the concept of *Battling for the Bounty*... make a list of some bounty you have gathered after a battle. Take a moment and thank God for bringing good things out of your most difficult battle.

How can *Battling for the Bounty* help you start thinking differently when you are in the heat of battle and want to give up?

Choose 3 ways you can encourage yourself in the Lord while you are facing the enemy. This will prove to be important when you're in the heat of the battle. We don't want to react in fear while in battle. When you know your response, you have what's called *resolve*. Look that word up in the dictionary and see if you have it. When we react, we allow our feelings to dictate our response instead of relying on our resolve. The question is: will we fall prey to our feelings or stand strong in our faith? These things must be decided *before* the battle begins.

BECOMING STATEMENTS

God doesn't waste a thing. He uses every weapon used against me to build strength, stamina, and confidence deep within my soul.

There's bounty in every battle!

BELIEVING THE BIBLE

For every child of God defeats this evil world, and we achieve this victory through our faith. 1 John 5:4 (NLT)

The weapons that
once wounded
become
the kindling
that sets our
heart
ablaze

Troubles
today
are
territories
of
triumph
tomorrow

THE VICTORY GIRL

The King's daughter is all glorious within. Psalm 45:13 NASB

Becoming a *Victory Girl* is a reason to celebrate. Sweet girl, we've learned to relish in the bounty of our battles and celebrate in triumph over our enemy. I want you to do a little happy dance because you've learned how to take back your God-given territory. I especially want to celebrate *you*! You've made your way onto the battlefields of Life with Jesus at your side.

I hope you've begun taking God at His Word about your destiny. And, I hope you are planning on staking your claim in The Kingdom of God. He's got a special place in mind for you! It's your Good Land. Get out there and defend your territory because it's got your name written all over it! Let the enemy know he's messing with a daughter of the King and the King's got your back! Send the enemy running in fear because you know you are a *Victory Girl*!

Becoming a *Victory Girl* is hard work.

Maybe you feel like no one has even noticed your hard-fought battles and well-deserved victories. Please hear this! When it feels like you're invisible, you can be sure the King sees. God knows every battle you've fought to become fully His. He knows every scar, every wound, every shattered piece of your heart. He even knows every tear you've cried.

You've kept track of all my wandering and my weeping. You've stored my many tears in your bottle…The very moment I call to you for a Father's help the tide of battle turns and my enemies flee! This one thing I know: God is on my side! Psalm 56:8 (TPT)

The *Victory Girl* has one proud Papa! Sweet girl, He's so proud of you and I am too! You are a daughter of the King. Did your spirit hear that? Listen! Don't be scared. In the middle of a battle, you've got a powerful Papa. You're no longer a slave to fear, but a child of the Most High God. You've got access to the throne. Don't be afraid to ask Him for what you need. Yes, we'll have ongoing battles, but we fight with supernatural weapons. While the battle rages on, we stand!

You see, you have not received a spirit that returns you to slavery, so you have nothing to fear. The Spirit you have received adopts you and welcomes you into God's own family. That's why we call out to Him, "Abba! Father!" as we would address a loving daddy. Through that prayer, God's Spirit confirms in our spirits that we are His children. If we are God's children, that means we are His heirs along with the Anointed, set to inherit everything that is His. If we share His sufferings, we know that we will ultimately share in His glory. Now I'm sure of this: the sufferings we endure now are not even worth comparing to the glory that is coming and will be revealed in us. Romans 8:15-18 (VOICE)

The *Victory Girl* gets a crown!

Victory Girl, you've even been given a crown...in fact you are a crown in His hand. No longer forsaken, but called His own. No longer empty, but filled with His Spirit. He delights in you because you are His! You have a crown, wear it!

And you will be the crowning glory of the Eternal's power, a royal crown cradled in His palm and held aloft by your God for all to see. People won't talk about you anymore using words like "forsaken" or "empty." Instead, you will be called "My delight" and the land around you "Married," because the Eternal is pleased with you and has bound Himself to your land.
Isaiah 62:3-4 (VOICE)

He even knows your name! You have nothing to fear when you're one of His daughters! You are precious in His sight and He is crazy about you!

Daughter of the King...always wear your invisible crown!

"Do not fear, for I have redeemed you; I have called you by name; you are Mine! When you pass through the waters, I will be with you; and through the rivers, they will not overflow you. When you walk through the fire, you will not be scorched, nor will the flame burn you. For I am the Lord your God, the Holy One of Israel, your Savior...Since you are precious in My sight, since you are honored and I love you...Do not fear, for I am with you..."
Isaiah 43:1-5 (NASB)

Come bravely before His throne. Hebrews 4:16 (CEB)

You will be a crown of beauty in the hand of the Lord. Isaiah 62:3 (ESV)

Ask for what you need. He doesn't mind a bit. In fact, He encourages us to be brave and come boldly. Once you've asked Him, trust Him to provide all that you need. He's a good, good Father and He loves to give us what we need. Sometimes, He even gives us what we want, especially when our hearts our aligned with His. He gives us our heart's desires because they are His desires too. I want you to know, as His *Victory Girl*, you are encouraged, empowered, and equipped with everything you need for eternity and in this life too.

For Jesus is not some high priest who has no sympathy for our weaknesses and flaws. He has already been tested in every way that we are tested; but He emerged victorious, without failing God. So let us step boldly to the throne of grace, where we can find mercy and grace to help when we need it most.
Hebrews 4:15-16 (VOICE)

I want you to walk away from this book feeling truly encouraged, empowered, and equipped. I hope I've convinced you that you have everything you need to become a *Victory Girl*. But, maybe you're still dreaming of what it would be like to walk in victory. If your not quite convinced, that's okay, because guess what? Dreams do come true! The truth is, you're already a *Victory Girl*, whether you believe it or not, whether you feel like it or not, whether anyone else knows it or sees it. Even if you can't see it yet, He sees the future you! In fact, He says, because you're His daughter, you are beautiful and glorious!

The King's daughter is all glorious within. Psalm 45:13 (NASB)

VICTORY VIEWS: God made you a *Victory Girl*! He made you glorious. Now walk this thing out! Walk in your full destiny and who He made you to be. Let me say it again…*Victory Girl*, you are glorious! The *Victory Girl* looks out over her God-given territory with a sense of belonging, a fullness of joy, and a new-found confidence in her authority, knowing she's a daughter of the King.

YOU ARE HIS *VICTORY GIRL*!

I found the perfect Psalm to seal up everything the King has declared. There is no better way to close than with a Psalm of praise to our King. Right now, all I want to do is thank God for who He is and all He's done. And, I bet you do too! I've so enjoyed our time together. Keep it up girl, read this book again and again until you are convinced of what He says about you. And, when the truth has finally sunk in, please do me the favor of sharing what you've learned with someone else who needs to know they're His *Victory Girl* too! Do a Bible study together, give this book as a gift, and let me know what wonderful things He has done in your life. Would you please read the following Psalm as a prayer to the One who's made you a *Victory Girl*! All honor and glory and praise to our King Jesus!

CLOSING PRAYER:

The very moment I call to you for a Father's
help the tide of battle turns
and my enemies flee!
This one thing I know: God is on my side!
I trust in the Lord. And I praise Him!
I trust in the Word of God. And I praise Him!
What harm could man do to me?
With God on my side I will not be
afraid of what comes. My heart overflows
with praise to God and for His promises,
I will always trust in Him.
So I'm thanking You with all my heart,
with gratitude for all You've done.
I will do everything I've promised You, Lord.
For You have saved my soul from death
and my feet from stumbling so that
I can walk before the Lord bathed in His
life-giving light.
Psalm 56: 9-13 (TPT)

BATTLING IT OUT

The Victory Girl is our final chapter of *Becoming a Victory Girl: Staking Your Claim in The Kingdom*. Do you feel like a *Victory Girl*? If not, let me tell you again; whether you believe it or not, you are His *Victory Girl*. Keep speaking His Truth over yourself. Ask Him to help you believe what He says about you. Because, *Victory Girl*, it's true!

How can *The Victory Girl* help you to better understand your identity in Christ? Daughter of the King, always wear your invisible crown!

Is there someone you know who needs to learn how to become a *Victory Girl* too? Share your journey of becoming a *Victory Girl* with someone today. Invite them to coffee; give them a copy of this book. Ask them to help you keep your land and walk in your God-given destiny. Be willing to help them do the same. Dream big with God! And when necessary, call in the reinforcements…ask your friends to help you keep your brave on.

Choose 3 ways you're going to live out being *a Victory Girl*.

Write out *The Victory Girl Manifesto*, put it somewhere you can see it, say it out loud, rewrite it in your journal, and memorize it. Remembering how God sees you will help you remain confident about being a *Victory Girl*. Say *The Victory Girl Manifesto* out loud the next time you're not feeling confident about the work God's done in your heart through *Becoming a Victory Girl*. I know He's done it; don't you forget it! We can't walk away from being in His Presence and remain unchanged. The very nearness of Him does something to our hearts. Whether by His Word or by His Spirit…we will be changed.

BECOMING STATEMENTS

The *Victory Girl* is encouraged, empowered, and equipped with everything she needs for eternity and everyday life too. I am a *Victory Girl*.

BELIEVING THE BIBLE

For You clothed me with strength for the battle. Psalm 18:39 (MEV)

THE
VICTORY
GIRL
ALWAYS
WEARS
HER
INVISIBLE
CROWN

The Victory Girl Manifesto:
The Victory Girl
looks out over her
God-given territory
with a sense of
belonging,
a fullness of joy, &
a new-found confidence
in her authority,
knowing she's a
daughter of the King.

A FINAL NOTE

Throughout this book, we've walked through God's strategies to help you begin the journey of *Becoming a Victory Girl: Staking Your Claim in The Kingdom*. My hope is that as you find yourself on the final page of this book, you are walking away feeling victorious, refreshed, passionate, and poised in the pursuit of your enemies. I really hope you're feeling a little invincible! My prayer is that you are holding your head high, knowing God, who is called Faithful and True, really is Who He says He is! Let me just say, "Victory Girl, you've got this!"

Remember you have everything you need to be victorious.
Practice these *Victory Girl Skills* because now you know how to:

* Wage warfare and train for triumph as a *Warrior of Victory*.
* Pray with power, authority, and accuracy, hitting the mark every time through mastering *The Art of the Aim*.
* Stake, claim and keep the territory you've conquered through *Staking Your Claim in the Kingdom*.
* Bask in the spoils of victory, do a happy dance, and sing your praises loudly while *Battling for the Bounty*.

You are equipped to walk in your full authority knowing these things:

* You have an Inheritance and Identity in Christ
* God's really fighting your battles
* You are a daughter of the King

Most importantly, I pray you know and believe you are
His *Victory Girl*!

ABOUT THE AUTHOR

Amy Elaine Martinez is an inspirational speaker, author, gifted teacher, radio show host and ministry leader. Married for twenty-five years to the love of her life, David, she's also the proud boy-mom of Sidney and Gabriel. Recently, their family grew with the blessing of a daughter-in-love, Sidney's wife, Riley, and their Aussie named Maverick.

A storyteller at heart, Amy Elaine loves to share how she became a *Victory Girl* through the transforming power of the Holy Spirit. She humbly bears the scars of a broken life and it's her heart's desire to see women walk in wholeness and live in victory. In fact, *Becoming a Victory Girl* is a vital part of how she found a deeper healing in her life.

Turning everyday moments into an extraordinary life motivates Amy Elaine to share her journey of becoming whole again with the broken, bruised, and bound every time she gets the chance. Most days you'll find her writing at a coffee shop or ministering across the table to a friend. Amy lives part-time in Castle Rock, Colorado, and recently moved to Guthrie, Oklahoma.

A graduate of Oklahoma Baptist University, she has a BA in sociology. Amy Elaine serves in various ministries, has an active speaking calendar, blogs frequently on her website where she is helping heart-shattered lives become whole again through Christ.

She'd love to hear from you. To contact Amy Elaine, subscribe to the blog to receive her devotionals, keep up-to-date with what's going on at Amy Elaine Ministries, or invite her to speak at your next women's event, please visit her website at AmyElaine.com.

You can follow Amy Elaine on social media here:

Facebook: @amyelainewrites
Twitter: @amyelainewrites
Instagram: @amyelainewrites
Website: https://www.amyelaine.com
YouTube: Amy Elaine Ministries
Itunes: Amy Elaine Ministries
SoundCloud: Amy Elaine Ministries

REAL VICTORY RADIO SHOW

Amy Elaine Ministries is proud to announce the addition of *Real Victory Radio* on 94.7 FM The Word KRKS in the Denver area. Live streaming is available by downloading the app to listen anywhere! Amy Elaine shares how to get REAL: Ready & Equipped for an Authentic Life of Victory! With special guests, author interviews, and Biblical teaching, you will be encouraged to be strong and courageous.

Many of us bear the scars of a broken life, but long to find wholeness again. On *Real Victory Radio*, you'll hear how Jesus can help you pick up the pieces of your shattered life- just like He did for me - and how His transforming power can lead you to live in REAL VICTORY every day. Please join us for *Real Victory Radio* every Saturday live or by using the app. If you miss us live, you can always catch the replay on the Amy Elaine Ministries *YouTube* Channel.

Join the **Victory Movement** with *Real Victory Radio*

We'd love to have you partner with us in our radio ministry outreach to help encourage listeners to walk in wholeness and live in REAL VICTORY as we share the Gospel of Jesus Christ. Amy Elaine Ministries, Inc. is a non-profit organization.

You can join our *Victory Movement* and help get the Word out through Real Victory Radio. If you're interested in making a tax-deductible donation through our website, You can choose to make a single donation or become a Monthly Partner. Your generous donations help us to continue to share the love of God with our listeners so they can live a life of REAL VICTORY.

A HOPE-FULL NOTE BY AMY ELAINE

Thank you for your interest in partnering with me to help reach the broken, bruised, and bound. More than anything, I'd love for you to pray with me for the ministry of Real Victory Radio. The prayer of my heart is for God to meet the needs of those who listen in a mighty way just like He did in my own life. This ministry exists to bind up the broken-hearted and be an encouragement by offering renewed hope to every woman longing to become whole again. God did it for me and I know He longs to help others become a broken girl made whole too!

Please prayerfully consider how you can grow the Kingdom by coming alongside this ministry by partnering with Amy Elaine Ministries. Thank you for your continued prayers. It's our heart to see lives changed through Jesus and the transforming power of the Holy Spirit. He, alone, is our Hope. He is the Hope for broken lives.

Isaiah 61:1 reminds us that, "The Spirit of the Sovereign LORD is upon me, for the LORD has anointed me to bring good news to the poor. He has sent me to comfort the brokenhearted and to proclaim that captives will be released and prisoners will be freed."

Walking in wholeness & living in victory through Jesus~

Amy Elaine Martinez

51475038R00039

Made in the USA
Columbia, SC
23 February 2019